Enter to Worship – Exit to Serve

By Ronald K. Gray

Copyright © 2008 by Ronald K. Gray

Enter to Worship – Exit to Serve
by Ronald K. Gray

Printed in the United States of America

ISBN 9781470091286

Acknowledgements:

I am thankful to the Lord for allowing me to proclaim the Gospel for over 34 years. It has brought great joy and has been a privilege for me.

I am grateful to my wife, Sharon, who has stood with me as we have taken steps of faith to minister to others. She has been my encourager and support. I love her dearly.

Charles Simpson has been a great friend and pastor to me. His guidance has been invaluable.

Thanks to:

Carl Wren for his help with editing.

Our faithful financial supporters who help us fulfill our calling

To my family and friends who have shared in my many and varied roles of ministry through the years.

Index

Enter to worship

Introduction

For the children of Israel and the children of Levi shall bring the offering of the corn, of the new wine, and the oil, unto the chambers, where are the vessels of the sanctuary, and the priests that minister, and the porters, and the singers: and we will not forsake the house of our God.
Nehemiah 10:39 King James Version

Most of us who have been in church for any length of time know the story of Nehemiah. From the king's court in Susa, capitol of Persia, God's exiled prophet heard that the walls of Jerusalem had crumbled and that its inhabitants had been scattered abroad. The city was in chaos. The walls were broken down. The temple was in ruins. Nothing was happening there, and nobody seemed to care.

The God of Israel was not being worshiped in spirit and in truth. Nehemiah felt compelled by the Spirit of God to go back to Jerusalem. He went at great personal risk, but the rebuilding of the walls and the restoration of the temple were more important that any personal consideration.

Sins of rebellion and idolatry had caused spiritual dearth in the land. The affairs of God must always be put ahead of the affairs of man, and Nehemiah was the voice God would use to call His people back to worship. He knew that the reason the walls had crumbled and the children of Israel had been dispersed was because they had forsaken the house of the Lord. *They had ceased to worship God as He had ordained.*

During the twentieth year of the reign of King Artaxerxes I (464-424 B. C.) Hanani, a brother, and other Judean men visited Susa. These men reported the affliction and reproach of the remnant of Jews from Babylonian captivity in Jerusalem and its state of disrepair (Nehemiah 1:2, 3). This news distressed Nehemiah, cup bearer of King Artaxerxes. He wept, mourned, fasted and addressed God with the following prayer:

And I said: "I pray, LORD God of heaven, O great and awesome God, You who keep Your covenant and mercy with those who love You and observe Your commandments, please let Your ear be attentive and Your eyes open, that You may hear the prayer of Your servant which I pray before You now, day and night, for the children of Israel Your servants, and confess the sins of the children of Israel which we have sinned against You. Both my father's house and I have sinned. We have acted very corruptly against

*You, and have not kept the commandments, the stat-
utes, nor the ordinances which You commanded Your
servant Moses. Remember, I pray, the word that You
commanded Your servant Moses, saying, 'If you are
unfaithful, I will scatter you among the nations; but
if you return to Me, and keep My commandments
and do them, though some of you were cast out to
the farthest part of the heavens, yet I will gather
them from there, and bring them to the place which I
have chosen as a dwelling for My name.' Now these
are Your servants and Your people, whom You have
redeemed by Your great power, and by Your strong
hand. O Lord, I pray, please let Your ear be attentive
to the prayer of Your servant, and to the prayer of
Your servants who desire to fear Your name; and let
Your servant prosper this day, I pray, and grant him
mercy in the sight of this man."*

For I was the king's cup bearer. (Nehemiah 1:5-11)

After a period of mourning, Nehemiah petitioned
the King for support in reconstructing the walls
and gates of Jerusalem. Artaxerxes commissioned
Nehemiah to the governership of the required task.

Chapters 1 through 7 note the successful recon-
struction of the walls and the gates. However,
Nehemiah's job was not complete. Sin was the root
of the broken state of God's people. Nehemiah, in
his prayer of repentance, pointed out particular sins:
failing to keep the commandments, statutes, and rules
that were a vital part of the Holy Covenant.

In chapter 8, the law was read to Israel at the
Water Gate (1-8). Thus, the Water Gate served as

a place of cleansing through the hearing of God's word. The word brought a spiritual revival in chapter 9 (1-37). The people confessed their sins and began to pray.

The act of repentance was useless without the commitment to fulfill the obligations of the Holy Covenant. Hearing of the word and spiritual revival fosters true worship of God. In chapter 10, it is noted that Israel made a written covenant, physical and spiritual, with each other and with God to return to the holy rituals of worship.

For example, Nehemiah said that all Israel should bring their sacrifices and their offerings to God in the presence of priests, porters and singers. However, the most powerful statement is reserved for the last sentence of the 39th verse:

"and we will not neglect the house of our God."

This should be the cry of God's children today. The House of the Lord should be priority in every believer's life.

Faithfulness to God's House does not mean limitation to a particular building or group. God insists that His people be faithful to the dwelling place of His Spirit. 1 Corinthians 6:19-20 tells us:

Or do you not know that your body is the temple of the Holy Spirit *who is* in you, whom you have from God, and you are not your own? For you were bought at a price; therefore glorify God in your body and in your spirit, which are God's.

The children of God, bought by the precious blood of Jesus Christ, are the house of God. We serve as His dwelling place. Individually, Christians represent the body of Christ. Corporately, the body represents the church and the bride. Therefore, there is no room for idols in a Christian's life. 2 Corinthians 6:16 says:

And what agreement has the temple of God with idols? For you are the temple of the living God. As God has said:
"I will dwell in them
And walk among them.
I will be their God,
And they shall be My people."

The House of the Lord is anywhere, anytime Christians gather in the Name of Jesus Christ. And He blesses unity.

From the word of the Lord, it is evident that God expects His people to keep His commandments, statutes and rules. Failure to worship God in spirit and truth makes the personal covenant with Him void (e.g. the sinful state of the children of Israel). Therefore, it is essential for the Christian to understand the significance and the opportunities to worship God and then put into service what has been accomplished.

I believe that this teaching will help many of us understand why we don't get more out of church life than we do. Some of us leave defeated and we shouldn't. Some of us feel as though nothing happened. It is not God's fault. I believe that we get out of worship what we put into it.

Whatever we expect from God is what we receive from Him. If we expect great things, we will receive great things.

We cannot have the attitude to simply ask God's blessings in our life. That is a tendency of the church today. We should desire to actively participate in a relationship with Him. Our lives should show sacrifice to Him. We enter to worship Him and exit to serve Him in all our ways.

.

Enter to Worship

Chapter 1:

The Offering of the Corn

"The children of Israel and the children of Levi shall bring the offering of the corn . . ."

Nehemiah 10:39 KJV

Worship always means sacrifice. That is the way of God. That is His plan. Nehemiah told the people of Israel to bring their gifts to God when they came to worship Him. They were to bring corn, new wine and oil.

Corn is translated in many versions of the Scripture as "grain". In Old Testament times, they did not have a developed currency system. They used a barter system, exchanging their sacks of grain for whatever materials they needed. Grain for chickens or grain for sugar. Today we use dollars, debit cards and credit cards. We don't want you to bring sacks of grain today, we use currency.

Many cultures, including ours, have used this system through the years. Grain equaled money, so when they brought their offering of grain, they were bringing an offering of their material goods—the same as we do with money.

The Lord is interested in money! There are about 500 verses of scripture on prayer and over 2300 verses on how to handle money. I believe that this scripture in Nehemiah is indicative of a theme that runs through all of scripture. If we don't know how to handle money or unwilling to give money, then we will not be able to accomplish anything else for God. Luke 16:1-13 spells this out very clearly:

He also said to His disciples: "There was a certain rich man who had a steward, and an accusation was brought to him that this man was wasting his goods. So he called him and said to him, 'What is this I hear about you? Give an account of your stewardship, for you can no longer be steward.'

"Then the steward said within himself, 'What shall I do? For my master is taking the stewardship away from me. I cannot dig; I am ashamed to beg. I have resolved what to do, that when I am put out of the stewardship, they may receive me into their houses.'

"So he called every one of his master's debtors to him, and said to the first, 'How much do you owe my master?' And he said, 'A hundred measures of oil.' So he said to him, 'Take your bill, and sit down quickly and write fifty.' Then he said to another, 'And how much do you owe?' So he said, 'A hundred measures

of wheat.' And he said to him, 'Take your bill, and write eighty.' So the master commended the unjust steward because he had dealt shrewdly. For the sons of this world are more shrewd in their generation than the sons of light.

"And I say to you, make friends for yourselves by unrighteous mammon, that when you fail, they may receive you into an everlasting home. 10 He who is faithful in what is least is faithful also in much; and he who is unjust in what is least is unjust also in much. Therefore if you have not been faithful in the unrighteous mammon, who will commit to your trust the true riches? And if you have not been faithful in what is another man's, who will give you what is your own?

"No servant can serve two masters; for either he will hate the one and love the other, or else he will be loyal to the one and despise the other. You cannot serve God and mammon."

Money is a spiritual commodity. We want to excel in prayer, Bible reading, etc., but we struggle with money. Money represents our time. We work 40 hours a week for a paycheck. The paycheck represents the value of our time. Not one of us would work those hours for free, but we use the money to pay bills and invest in our future.

Why is it that in so many churches, when we talk about money, people struggle? It is said so often that all the church does is talk about money, but that is not true. The percentage of time that the majority of churches spend talking about this very important matter is far less that most other topics. One pastor where I ministered stood up and said, "We don't talk about money in our church." He seemed to feel that was a positive thing. The truth is that preaching concerning money is just as anointed as John 3:16. It is the Word of God.

We need a theology of money. We have learned scriptures on healing, deliverance, salvation and the Holy Spirit, but most have not learned many scriptures on money. We cannot pretend that these scriptures don't exist. The truth is that if we don't deal with our finances, they will deal with us.

The first place to begin is Psalm 24:1: *"The earth is the Lord's and all its fullness, the world and those who dwell therein."* We must know that everything belongs to God and we are stewards. The main issue is ownership.

In Ecclesiastes 5:19 Solomon says: *"As for every man to whom God has given riches and wealth, and given him power to eat of it, to receive his heritage and rejoice in his labor—this is the gift of God."* And in Matthew 6:19-21 Jesus says, *"Do not lay up for yourselves treasures on earth, where moth and rust destroy and where thieves break in and steal; but lay up for yourselves treasures in heaven, where neither moth nor rust destroys and where thieves do not break in and steal. For where your treasure is, there your heart will be also."*

Are we willing to change? Are we hoarding treasure, "a stock of valuables in reserve" for ourselves, or are we committed to the fact that we serve God and He is able to take care of us?

The truth is that we can become slaves to money. The word serve is used twice in Matthew 6:24: *"No one can serve two masters; for either he will hate the one and love the other, or else he will be loyal to the one and despise the other. You cannot serve God and mammon."* Here "serve" means "slave", either voluntarily or involuntarily.

The question is not one of advisability. It does not say "you should not." That would be a priority choice. It is not a question of accountability. It does not say "you must not." That would be a moral choice. Rather it is a matter of impossibility. "You can not." We are either a slave to money or God.

In our theology of money, we either have a poverty mentality, prosperity mentality or a stewardship mentality. A poverty mentality has a disdain for possessions. They are a curse. There is a preoccupation with daily needs.

A prosperity mentality believes that money is the reward of the righteous. They believe it is the right of the Christian. There is an idea of transactions, like an ATM machine.

A stewardship mentality believes that money is a trust given in various proportions. It is a privilege given from the hand of the Lord. A steward prays for wisdom on how to carry out the will of the Father, using the finances that have been given him.

There are four primary areas of financial giving.

1. Tithes: The main argument about tithes is that it is an Old Testament Law principle. The truth is that it is a principle instituted by God that predates the law. In Genesis 14, Abraham pays a tithe to Melchezidek, the high priest of Salem. This was 500 years before the law was given to Moses. In Genesis 28:22 Jacob promised to give God one-tenth of all his increase. This was 400 years before the Law.

The fact is that Jesus said in Matthew 23:23 that the Pharisees and scribes ought to pay tithes. They were not to obey part of the law but neglect the truth of tithing.

I believe that tithing is something we do because of the great investment God has made in us, His children. I Peter 2:9 proclaims that we are a peculiar people. The literal Greek means "a purchased possession." The word declares we are bought with a price, the precious Blood of Jesus Christ.

Tithing represents our belief that God owns us and will supply our every need. It represents a covenant with God.

We can trust God to do His part, but can He trust us to do our part? Many of the problems we have today can be attributed to our not tithing. When we do tithe, we show we believe God to be our source.

Many years ago I went to a church that had a factory in their city that employed many of the church people. They were struggling to deal with a serious problem. I asked the pastor if the majority of the church tithed. He said that they had been very faithful in that area. I stood before the church and declared to them that God would rebuke the devourer for their sake and that their vine would not cast its fruit before its season, based on Malachi 3.

In three days, another company came in and bought that factory and hired back every one of the employees at a better salary than before. I believe that tithing brings job security. The world is not our security. Tithing releases us into the economy of God. This is not about Old Testament versus New Testament. It is about Kingdom!

Malachi 3:8-12 says:

"Will a man rob God? Yet you have robbed Me! But you say, 'In what way have we robbed You?'

In tithes and offerings. You are cursed with a curse, for you have robbed Me, Even this whole nation. Bring all the tithes into the storehouse, that there may be food in My house. And try Me now in this," says the LORD of hosts, "If I will not open for you the windows of heaven and pour out for you such blessing that there will not be room enough to receive it. And I will rebuke the devourer for your sakes, so that he will not destroy the fruit of your ground. Nor shall the vine fail to bear fruit for you in the field," says the LORD of hosts; "and all nations will call you blessed, for you will be a delightful land," says the LORD of hosts.

Refusing to tithe brings a curse! ***Today, we are more concerned with bank robbers than God robbers***. I personally believe that if everyone in every church tithed, there would be enough money to build every building, support every missionary, and touch every person around the world with the Gospel. People say that they will pay their tithes when they have more money.

The truth is that if we don't tithe when we have a little, we won't tithe when we have a lot!

Now some people ask how we know whether people are tithing or not. We should check. When I was growing up, people said the preacher ought not to look at tithing records. He might be tempted to preach condemnation if he sees the people are not tithing.

It is amazing that most people want the preacher to identify sin as long as it is not theirs. As long as someone else is being talked about, it is okay. The truth is that a lack of tithing opens the door to satanic influence. If we believe that those called of God have a duty to set people free, then we must give them the freedom to check into tithe records. I have seen a marked difference in the lives of those who tithe to the Kingdom of God.

As a pastor I saw in counseling sessions the problems that came from robbing God. When the devourer is not rebuked, he has his way in people's lives.

I came across this story by James E. Carter in "A Sourcebook for Stewardship Sermons":

The day the church treasurer resigned the church, he asked the local grain elevator manager to take the position. The manager agreed under two conditions.

1. That no treasurer's report would be given for the first year.

2. That no questions be asked about finances during that year.

The people were surprised but finally agreed since most of them did business with him and he was a trusted man.

At the end of the year he gave his report:

The church indebtedness of $228,000 had been paid.

The minister's salary had been increased by 8 percent.

The Cooperative Program gifts have been paid 200 percent.

There were no outstanding bills.

There was a cash balance of $11,252!

Immediately the shocked congregation asked, "How did you do it? Where did the money come from?" He quietly answered: "Most of you bring your grain to my elevator. Throughout the year I simply withheld ten percent on your behalf and gave it to the church in your name. You didn't even miss it!"

"Do you see what we could do for the Lord if we were all willing to give at least the tithe to God, who really owns it?"

The new treasurer had made his point.

A lot of people leave a church because they say they are not being fed. Have any of you ever heard that? I am convinced that the primary reason they are not being fed is because they are not paying their tithes. You pay into the storehouse and the word promises there will be meat on the table.

Two people can be in the same service and hear the same message, but one leaves saying what a great word and the other says that it did not affect them.

Some people do not receive from the Word, because they have not invested anything into the storehouse.

Your tithe is given for the priesthood of the storehouse. It is used to bring about the plan of God. There are those today who want to own the tithe and use it for their own personal gain. The responsibility rests on the shoulders of the leadership God has set in the house of God.

There have been mistakes made and probably more will be made in the future. It weighs on the hearts of most leaders. We need wisdom for the responsibility God has given us.

When we give correctly, I believe it translates into anointing that rests upon the people of God. His desire is that we mature spiritually into what He desires us to be. My mind cannot comprehend it, but God does it.

We have a covenant with God that will bring about His purposes.

2. First Fruits. Deuteronomy 18:4 reads: *"The first fruits of your grain and your new wine and your oil, and the first of the fleece of your sheep, you shall give him."* Proverbs 3:9-10 reads:

Honor the LORD with your possessions,
And with the first fruits of all your increase;
So your barns will be filled with plenty,
And your vats will overflow with new wine.

This is an offering, not a tithe. God delights when we honor Him as He gives us increase. All my life

I have heard people declare how God has blessed them. They owe everything to Him. Those things are true, but we seem to have a problem in honoring God with an offering that says we really love him.

The problem is that we tend to tip God. We seek God for His blessings, but then feel that we have no responsibility to include Him in our rewards. We give a check made out to what we feel instead of an offering that says we honor God.

The only thing that limits our first fruit offerings is our faith. We should give to Him abundantly as He increases our lives.

3. Alms: Giving alms is close to God's heart. Acts 3:2-3 speaks of giving alms:

And a certain man lame from his mother's womb was carried, whom they laid daily at the gate of the temple which is called Beautiful, to ask alms from those who entered the temple; who, seeing Peter and John about to go into the temple, asked for alms.

Psalm 82:3 says:

Defend the poor and fatherless;
Do justice to the afflicted and needy.

And Psalm 41:1:

Blessed is he who considers the poor;
The LORD will deliver him in time of trouble.

Proverbs 19:17 reads:

He who has pity on the poor lends to the LORD,
And He will pay back what he has given.

When we give to the poor, we are truly showing the love of Jesus. When we give to the poor, God says he will repay us dollar for dollar. We will not receive a great increase of monies, but it blesses the heart of God.

It is so easy to become hardhearted in this world towards the poor. Granted, some of them are in their situations by choice, but the majority of poor are there because of difficulties they have faced.

I have been to some of the poorest countries in the world. Haiti, Mexico and the Democratic Republic of the Congo are countries that have faced many problems because of corrupt government and tribalism. People are caught in the middle of age-old wars and battles that they did not cause. These people need help. We must continually be open to help those who have less that what we have. I saw so many beggars in so many countries; I became deaf to their cries. It became easy for me to walk by them and not even see them. While there are certainly con men and women, the fact is that there are many who desperately need help. I passed by one women begging one day and the Spirit of the Lord spoke to me to stop and give her something. I felt God soften my heart. He let me know He would help me with His leading, if I would listen to Him. It is important to be sensitive to the Holy Spirit and listen to His voice.

Greed was listed as one of the Seven Deadly Sins, and continues to plague the church. When will we open our hearts and believe that God will sustain us?

It was never God's plan for the government to be the caretaker of the poor. We have a responsibility. God is still the God of more than enough.

There is a tendency in people to give the leftovers to the poor.

I understand that a little. When I first started traveling, churches would give me a grocery shower. This was to provide food for my family for the week I was there. I got to the point I cringed when they said "grocery shower". They gave me old cans without labels. It was always a "surprise meal". It is bad to open up five cans without labels and for all of them to be English peas. That will test your attitude.

We should not just give our bad, out of date food and goods to the poor. We should truly bless those who have less than we have.

Years ago, I had gone to a conference and they advertised a banquet. I really wanted to go, but I had only ten dollars in my wallet and the banquet cost seven. I really believed God wanted me to go, so I went, thinking I could make it until the next church offering.

The Spirit of the Lord really blessed me at that banquet. Doors were opened and answers to prayers came. Then a miracle happened. The pastor across from me reached into his pocket and took out a twenty dollar bill and gave it to me. I said, "Praise the Lord".

About a year later, I saw this same pastor and he gave me another twenty dollars. I thought that this was great and started looking for him wherever I went. I saw him again at an airport and he gave me another twenty.

This time I really did not need it. I looked across the room and saw another traveling evangelist. He had that hungry look I knew so well. I gave the twenty to him. He started to cry and say something. I stopped him and said God sent it through someone else and I was just passing on the blessing.

There are many ways to give alms. We just need to keep passing on the blessings.

4. Planting Seed: 2 Corinthians 9:6-11 tells us:

But this I say: He who sows sparingly will also reap sparingly, and he who sows bountifully will also reap bountifully. So let each one give as he purposes in his heart, not grudgingly or of necessity; for God loves a cheerful giver. And God is able to make all grace abound toward you, that you, always having all sufficiency in all things, may have an abundance for every good work. As it is written:

" He has dispersed abroad,

He has given to the poor;

His righteousness endures forever."

Now may He who supplies seed to the sower, and bread for food, supply and multiply the seed you have sown and increase the fruits of your righteousness, while you are enriched in everything for all liberality, which causes thanksgiving through us to God.

We do not actually plant financial seeds until we reach eleven percent in our giving. The first ten percent is the tithe. This is the area we receive harvest in. It is a principle that runs throughout the scripture. Gen. 8:22 says, *"While the earth remains, seed time and harvest shall not cease." Many people eat their seed instead of planting it.*

Another verse says that God gives seed to the sower. That means to have more seed, there must of necessity be sowing. So many people want to hoard their finances, but God says we should plant in fertile ground. There are so many ministries doing great works today. Missionaries, evangelists and other organizations are making a difference in the all the world.

While the tithe belongs to your storehouse, the seed can be planted in many areas. This should not be given because you feel sorry for the ministry or they have told you a sad story that moves you.

The seed should be sown with a purpose. You are expecting a harvest. You want to give to a ministry that is doing something and has fruit that you can see. Don't be manipulated, but listen to the Spirit of God to direct you where to plant. Sometimes the harvest is quick and sometimes it may take a season, but it will come because that is the promise of the Father.

I want to tell you a couple of personal stories. In 1995, my family and I moved to Mobile, Alabama.

I had been a pastor in South Carolina for ten years but felt that God had spoken to me about traveling ministry again. I went ahead of my family to find a place to live.

I looked for two days at rental houses but could not find one that would meet our needs. My realtor and I met together and I decided to buy a house. The realtor asked what my income was. I told him that at the moment, I did not have an income because I was just starting again to live by offerings and support from churches and friends.

The only way for me to get a loan was to show proof of income. The director of the ministry I was working with said that the ministry would stand with me. He asked me an unusual question: How much did I believe I would make in the coming year? I prayed about it and felt that God was in this new endeavor and would take care of me, so I wrote down a figure that was ten percent more than the salary I had received at the church. We took that to the bank and I bought the house.

At the end of the next year, my salary was within $100 of the amount I had written! God is Good! I might also include the fact that my wife did not see the house until we moved in. It turned out the border in the new house was exactly the same as our old house and I had not even noticed. Thank God for His grace.

A few weeks after moving to Mobile, I was on my way to lunch with a friend and went by my office to pick up my support check. This was the check that was to cover our living expenses for the next two weeks. When I saw the small amount of the check, I was so discouraged. I could not believe how little money had come in.

All the way to lunch, I brooded. Finally, the Holy Spirit spoke to me: "Is your faith in that check or me?" I responded and said, my faith was in the Lord. I threw the check in the back seat and turned on some praise music and began to lift my voice to the Lord.

While I was having lunch with my friend, he suddenly stopped eating and looked me in the eyes and asked me if I could use $2000 for the ministry. I almost passed out. I said yes. He wrote me a check and went back to eating. I stayed calm on the outside, but inside I was jumping up and down. We had been friends for many years and he had never done that before. It was a miracle.

The final story is that I had sown some money into several ministries and was praying about some needs that we had. My youngest daughter needed a vehicle to drive. We really did not have the money, but I told her we would trust the Lord. A friend of mine went with me on a mission trip and during one of our conversations, I told him I was praying for the money for a car for our daughter. Nothing else was said.

A few weeks after returning home, he called and said he was giving us a Jeep Grand Cherokee for her. What a blessing.

God provides for us in so many ways. He truly is the provider. My wife and I give our tithes, offering and alms, and sow seeds. We give more than the ten percent. I want to move into another realm. Don't limit God. Trust Him with your finances, and allow Him to bless you with every blessing He has.

The Word says, *"A good man leaves an inheritance to his children's children: and the wealth of the sinner is laid up for the just."* I believe God wants us to walk humbly before Him in obedience. He will help us in the midst of every situation.

Chapter 2:

The Offering of the New Wine

For the children of Israel and the children of Levi shall bring the offering . . . of the new wine
Nehemiah 10:39 KJV

In rebuilding the temple, Nehemiah restored the spiritual relationship of the children of Israel with God Almighty. As they grew closer to God, they made a covenant one with another, and they said, "We will not forsake the House of our God." They signed their names to a piece of parchment and said, "We agree to this." And they began to make sacrifices and to worship Him.

One of the offerings was the new wine. The new wine is symbolic of the abundant life. Jesus explains in Mark 2:19-22:

> *And Jesus said to them, "Can the friends of the bridegroom fast while the bridegroom is with them? As long as they have the bridegroom with them they cannot fast. But the days will come when the bridegroom will be taken away from them, and then they will fast in those days.*
>
> *No one sews a piece of unshrunk cloth on an old garment; or else the new piece pulls away from the old, and the tear is made worse. And no one puts new wine into old wineskins; or else the new wine bursts the wineskins, the wine is spilled, and the wineskins are ruined. But new wine must be put into new wineskins."*

The abundant life is symbolized by the fruit of the Spirit given in Galatians 5:22-23:

> *But the fruit of the Spirit is love, joy, peace, long-suffering, gentleness, goodness, faith, meekness, temperance: against such there is no law.*

The fruit of the Spirit is the manifestation of the life of Christ within us. Everyone who is part of the Vine should be a partaker, and should be producing the fruit of the abundant life.

The manifestation of the flow of God in our lives is fruitfulness. We should not desire the old, but should desire the new. The new wine that bubbles forth can't be put into old wineskins. When the new wine starts to ferment, it starts to expand. If the wineskin is old, it is stiff and brittle and will burst.

The Lord's desire is that as new creations, we act in new ways with the overflow of His Spirit. He wants us to be producers of fruit so that the world will see something in our lives that causes them to want to move toward God.

A tree does not produce fruit just for looks. God doesn't make fruit just to be pretty either. I love to walk in fruit orchards. Apple, pear, orange and peach trees are beautiful when they are laden with fruit, but they are not just to be looked at. They are to be eaten.

When we come together as the people of God, we are to bring the abundant life of God, the fruit of the Spirit, with us. We are not to come together just to "look pretty."

Sometimes the church has fallen into a trap of thinking it is all about how we are seen. The truth is that the purpose is to bring something to the times of communion that will bless others. That is our primary purpose. We should have something to share.

We claim to have abundance, so we should be able to give to others. That is not just money and time. It is the good gifts that God puts in our hearts.

So many times we talk a good game but are not really bearing the fruit that God wants us to bear. The reason that people are not breaking down the doors to our churches to get in is that they don't want what we have. They see something in us that repels them instead of drawing them.

The church has lost it's influence on the world. We are not just marginalized, we are excluded. The issue is whether or not we truly live our lives according to His word.

I love to pick peaches. The primary reason I love to pick them is because I get to eat while I am picking. Sometimes I am not sure whether or not I am picking more or eating more.

A number of years ago I was picking some peaches in the Peach State, Georgia. I had peach juice all over me. I was about to quit, when I saw the biggest peach I had ever seen. I said, "I've got to have that peach," but it was on a limb that was just out of reach.

I wanted that peach so badly that finally I jumped as high as I could and grabbed it. When I did, I was surprised to realize that what looked so good on the front was rotten on the back. It was nasty! All of that nasty ran down my hand. When I think about it, I can still feel all that gooey stuff running down my hands even now. It took away my peach appetite.

Sometimes we come into our times of fellowship with everything looking good from one perspective. People don't see all of our hidden motives, desires and sins. We say all the right things. I have heard it said that most of us speak "Christianese".

We should have something to share with the body of Christ that is beneficial. Have you ever gone to church with a touch of the "blues," and someone comes up to you and begins to talk to you about the joy of the Lord? All of a sudden the "blues' disappear. What happened? You picked their fruit.

Another problem the church has today is that it has come to feel that the pastor or paid ministers are the ones to do the ministering. That is a lie. God calls for us to share what he has given us. This is not something to give Him, but to give one another.

It is a joy for someone who seems so sad to come up to me, but after talking they leave with a smile, because they have been able to pick my fruit. So many people go home unfulfilled after a service at church because they have been only spectators. We are here to bring something to the house of God that will build up His people.

Jesus gave a tough warning to anyone who says they don't have anything to give. *"I am the true vine, and My Father is the vinedresser. Every branch in Me that does not bear fruit He takes away; and every branch that bears fruit He prunes, that it may bear more fruit."* (John 15:1-2)

If the branches do not produce fruit, the vine-dresser will cut them off and burn them. He prunes the good branches so that the tree will produce the best fruit for the Kingdom of God. These words are not there to fill space! This is a prophetic utterance for the church today.

We are grafted into the Vine and are supposed to look like the Vine and act like the Vine. When people see us, they should see Jesus! The nature of the branch is to produce fruit. That is the purpose of our creation.

This is not a popular idea in our time. We have bought into the idea that there are no consequences in the Christian life. Today there is such a lack of hunger and thirst among the people of God. Most just want to be "blessed" but do not understand that, instead, they are to be a blessing. Self has become the dominant force. The idea of giving your life for the Kingdom and others has become almost archaic.

The Bible says in Ephesians 4:27 to give no place to the devil. We give him place if we operate the way the world does. We wait to love until somebody loves us. Our joy depends on circumstances.

The fruit of the Spirit is not a result of what anyone is doing to us. It is a result of what God is doing in us. It should not matter what people are saying about us, or what they are doing to us.

The tendency is to become a person of reaction instead of action. Sometimes we look good on the outside but are rotten on the inside. We say all the right things but slander people behind their backs. We are not here to react or respond to the attitudes of the world. We are here to show the attitude of God. We do right no matter what happens against us.

I care for you whether or not you care for me. Agape love is the love that gives, even if it costs our lives. The scripture says in 2 Corinthians 3:2, "*You are our epistle written in our hearts, known and read by all men.*"

There is no question that most people have a bad view of the church. Statistics show that the church is failing in its task to share God's love. The question is, will we make a difference? The answer is that we will make a difference to the ones we encounter.

Many years ago, I came across a saying called "The Love Commitment," though I don't know the name of the author. It says, **"Brother, I want you to know I am committed to you. You'll never knowingly suffer at my hand. I'll never do or say anything knowingly to hurt you. I'll always, in every circumstance, seek to help and support** you. If you are down and I can lift you up, I'll do that. Anything that I have that you need, I'll share it with you. And, if need be, I'll give it to you. No matter what happens in the future, either good or bad, my commitment to you will never change, and there is nothing you can do about it. You don't have to respond. I love you and that's what love means."

Here are some thoughts about the Fruit of the Spirit.

— **The Fruit of the Spirit is singular**. This suggests oneness and unity. It is one cluster on one stem of one vine. The vine, branch and stem just need to be healthy to grow.

— **Fruit grows and matures**. You can't obtain fruit by going to conferences or seminars. Nothing can instantly make you joyful, gentle or longsuffering. If we knew of such a place, we all know someone we would send.

— **Sometimes fruit trees require severe treatment to be fruit bearing.** It is the dry season that causes the roots to go deep, but causes the tree to have great stability.

— **Fruit trees require pruning**. God wants us to be fruitful, but He knows that there are some areas of our lives which take but do not produce. The Lord cuts those things away for our fruitfulness to reach full potential. Only weeds grow without cultivation.

— **The Fruit of the Spirit is a representation of the maturity of believers and the development**

of character in them. Gifts do not necessarily mean the approval of God. The Corinthian church exercised gifts without love. Where fruit is absent, gifts become practically worthless.

We must present ourselves to the Lord as willing sacrifices to become what He wants. May God help us to be a conduit of His love in this world.

Chapter 3:

The Offering of the Oil

For the children of Israel and the children of Levi shall bring the offering . . . of the oil
Nehemiah 10:39 KJV

Oil is used throughout the Scriptures to represent the Holy Spirit. When I first thought about that, all I could think of was, "How can we bring the Holy Spirit with us to give away, when He is in us all." In reality there is a **manifested presence** of the Holy Spirit that comes when we gather together to worship the Lord. God gives us gifts to share with one another when we assemble.

The body of Christ needs edification, exhortation and comfort. That is the purpose of the gifts. When the church functions as it was intended, people don't leave the church; they desire the benefits of His gifts.

What are the gifts? Let's look at what a church meeting should be from 1 Corinthians 12:7-31.

But the manifestation of the Spirit is given to each one for the profit of all: for to one is given the word of wisdom through the Spirit, to another the word of knowledge through the same Spirit, to another faith by the same Spirit, to another gifts of healing by the same Spirit, to another the working of miracles, to another prophecy, to another discerning of spirits, to another different kinds of tongues, to another the interpretation of tongues. But one and the same Spirit works all these things, distributing to each one individually as He wills.

For as the body is one and has many members, but all the members of that one body, being many, are one body, so also is Christ. 13 For by one Spirit we were all baptized into one body—whether Jews or Greeks, whether slaves or free—and have all been made to drink into one Spirit. For in fact the body is not one member but many.

If the foot should say, "Because I am not a hand, I am not of the body," is it therefore not of the body? And if the ear should say, "Because I am not an eye, I am not of the body," is it therefore not of the body? If the whole body were an eye, where would be the hearing? If the whole were hearing, where would be the smelling? But now God has set the members, each one of them, in the body just as He pleased. And if they were all one member, where would the body be?

But now indeed there are many members, yet one body. And the eye cannot say to the hand, "I have no need of you"; nor again the head to the feet, "I have no need of you." No, much rather, those members of the body which seem to be weaker are necessary. And those members of the body which we think to be less honorable, on these we bestow greater honor; and our unpresentable parts have greater modesty, 24 but our presentable parts have no need. But God composed the body, having given greater honor to that part which lacks it, that there should be no schism in the body, but that the members should have the same care for one another. And if one member suffers, all the members suffer with it; or if one member is honored, all the members rejoice with it.

Now you are the body of Christ, and members individually. And God has appointed these in the church: first apostles, second prophets, third teachers, after that miracles, then gifts of healing, helps, administrations, varieties of tongues. Are all apostles? Are all prophets? Are all teachers? Are all workers of miracles? 30 Do all have gifts of healing? Do all speak with tongues? Do all interpret? But earnestly desire the best gifts. And yet I show you a more excellent way.

And further, 1 Corinthians 14:23-26 tells us:

Therefore if the whole church comes together in one place, and all speak with tongues, and there come in those who are uninformed or unbelievers, will they not say that you are out of your mind? But if all prophesy, and an unbeliever or an uninformed person comes in, he is convinced by all, he is convicted by all. And thus the secrets of his heart are revealed; and so, falling down on his face, he will worship God and report that God is truly among you.

How is it then, brethren? Whenever you come together, each of you has a psalm, has a teaching, has a tongue, has a revelation, has an interpretation. Let all things be done for edification.

1 Corinthians 14:32-33 tells us, "*And the spirits of the prophets are subject to the prophets. For God is not the author of confusion but of peace, as in all the churches of the saints.*"

And 1 Corinthians 14:40 says, "*Let all things be done decently and in order.*"

I want to teach you a principle that God has shared with me in my life. I grew up with the idea that the spiritual gifts were not to be touched by common people. The only ones in the church that could be used in the gifts were the "spiritual" people.

The gifts were not something everyone could have or use. I was never taught the lesson to covet the gifts. What I heard said and what I gathered by watching was to not go into the area of spiritual gifts. If you misused the gifts, then God might hurt you. Now, I know the gifts are holy, but I also know that God intends for those gifts to be used to bring blessings to His church.

The truth is that the gifts are rarely taught and, therefore, are misunderstood by most people.

God wants His gifts to be understood and used by His people to bring maturity and blessing. The good news is that they are for everybody.

Even in the Old Testament in Nehemiah, it says that the children of Israel and the priests brought the oil. It was not just for the priesthood.

The Bible teaches we are all royal priests unto God. It also teaches that each of us is gifted. We have different gifts, but everyone has something to bring. If everyone brought their gift to the house of God, then all would be edified. We cannot let fear keep us from using our gifts.

There are some who feel that they are "God's policemen," who intimidate people with the idea that failure in the use of our gifts will bring punishment from God. We need rather to encourage one another.

You first need to believe you are gifted. You are useful to the Kingdom. Don't be afraid. The only way to learn is by doing. If you begin to use a gift and falter, then start again! Don't let the enemy rob you of the blessing of being used in the gift and giving others the benefit of that gift. There are a number of books today that teach Spiritual Gifts. I encourage you to read them and experiment.

I know this has some negative connotations for some, but sometimes we find what our true gifts are by finding out what gifts we don't have. God is our father. Sometimes we stumble and fall while we are learning. The good news is that He picks us up and holds us until we can walk again.

The Bible teaches about the gifts and gives some instructions, but they are not meant to detail every situation. The Holy Spirit teaches us that. After over 30 years of ministry, I have seen a multitude of things happen in churches that were not covered in any manual.

I once stopped two ladies in a church who were giving a message in tongues at the same time. When that had happened before, when I was young, it seemed the pastor and everybody else just kept their eyes closed and hoped that something else would happen. God spoke to me that both ladies had a valid word.

I stopped them and asked one of the ladies to give her message, then came an interpretation. Then I asked the other lady to give hers. When that interpretation came, God moved in a mighty way. Now that is not taught in most seminaries. You have to depend on the Spirit to give revelation to help you administer the gifts properly.

The key is, *do something*. Step out in faith!

God hates confusion! So many times, pastors just bow their heads and hope that things will turn out all right in the service instead of giving instruction. We have a responsibility to help people find their gifts, use them responsibly and bless the house of God.

We are to covet the best gifts. I believe that means the best gifts for the situation. Timing is everything. There are always gifts for each situation. I have seen pastors work out of experience and tradition instead of the Word and cause confusion.

One pastor gave a message in tongues after a prophecy came in the church. I asked him later why he did that. He said he needed to give the tongues to the interpretation. He completely misunderstood scripture and the understanding of prophecy.

We are not to be afraid of the gifts. The first time God used me, I thought I was going to faint because I could not breathe. People ask how do you know when you are going to give a word of the Lord. It is different for everyone. There is no set pattern. God will help you to know. He has a way of getting our attention.

Another issue is timing. We need to understand how God works in meetings and times of ministry. We try to force God or press our plans. Some things cannot be taught with a simplistic methodology. The primary way is being full of the Holy Spirit. He will guide us and help us to learn His ways.

God wants His church encouraged, exhorted and comforted. The gifts of the Spirit do this.

1 Corinthians 14:3 says, *"But he who prophesies speaks edification and exhortation and comfort to men." What would happen if everyone who came to a meeting used their spiritual gift? The body would be edified and comforted.*

It is not just for the preacher to bring his gift. Your gift is not invalid just because it does not include preaching.

We are not all hands or eyes. **We simply need to do what we are.**

1 Corinthians 14:26 reads, *"How is it then, brethren? Whenever you come together, each of you has a psalm, has a teaching, has a tongue, has a revelation, has an interpretation. Let all things be done for edification."*

We need to offer ourselves as vessels before God. We should have a willingness to be used by Him for His purposes. The tendency is to be spectators. We go to church, watch the preacher, listen to the singing, and wait for someone else to take the lead.

The gifts can be used anywhere the church is. That is not just behind four walls. We need to walk in the Spirit. Learn to pray more in the Spirit. Stop telling God what we can't do and start believing that we are useful for His service. Be a participant in the works of God. Start moving out by faith. Do something you have never done before. Wake up!

Chapter 4:

The Vessels

For the children of Israel and the children of Levi shall bring the offering (to) the vessels of the sanctuary Nehemiah 10:39 KJV

The vessels were in the temple to contain the offerings. When the priests and the people brought in their offerings, they poured them into vessels. Their worship was a gift to God. When we come into the House of God, we are to empty ourselves.

God wants to fill us to overflowing. Gifts are meant to continue on in people's lives, but we never give Him an opportunity, because we never empty ourselves of what He has given us before.

We are not here to say, "Bless me, Bless me," but to ask to be a blessing.

The Bible says it is more blessed to give than to receive. It also says if you give abundantly, you will receive abundantly. This applies not only to finances but to everything else as well. In Ezekiel and in the books of Samuel and Chronicles, when everything was in the temple as it was intended, the Glory filled the house. When we obey the Lord and come to His house and do as He requires, His glory will fill the temple.

This is the dynamic we desire. The Shekinah, the Cloud of Glory filling the house. Many churches today are empty of His presence. We have learned to do things in our own power. We have a set schedule and expect God and everyone else to live by our agenda and time table.

There are some churches that are being touched by a special presence of God. We should desire His touch more than anything else in our lives. It is not our plans that God wants. He wants our lives. He wants us to lay down our dreams and give Him opportunity to fill us with His purpose.

There is a story in 2 Kings 4 about a widow. The prophet told her to bring out all her pots and he would fill them. She borrowed pots from everyone she knew. She was only limited in her supply by how many pots she could bring. With the same enthusiasm, we need to bring all our empty lives to God for Him to fill.

I desire to Enter to Worship Him and give Him everything so that I can become a vessel to be filled again, and Exit to Serve Him. May His Glory fill His temple once again!

Exit To Serve

Chapter 5:

The Priests

. . .and the priests that minister

Nehemiah 10:39

The priests had two main functions in the Old Testament. The first was to offer sacrifices for all the children of Israel. They offered the blood of goats, turtledoves, lambs, sheep and bulls. The priests were set apart for this job.

They were also to proclaim the word of God. I don't find many occasions where they shared through expositional preaching. Instead they would take the sacred parchments and read what "thus says the Lord" over and over until it was instilled in the hearts and minds of the people and they knew what God was saying.

Today, some people think that preachers preach for a long time. Sometimes these priests would read for hours. When one priest got tired, another would take his place.

Nehemiah 8:1-8 reads:

When the seventh month came, the children of Israel were in their cities.

Now all the people gathered together as one man in the open square that was in front of the Water Gate; and they told Ezra the scribe to bring the Book of the Law of Moses, which the LORD had commanded Israel. So Ezra the priest brought the Law before the assembly of men and women and all who could hear with understanding on the first day of the seventh month. Then he read from it in the open square that was in front of the Water Gate from morning until midday, before the men and women and those who could understand; and the ears of all the people were attentive to the Book of the Law.

So Ezra the scribe stood on a platform of wood which they had made for the purpose; and beside him, at his right hand, stood Mattithiah, Shema, Anaiah, Urijah, Hilkiah, and Maaseiah; and at his left hand Pedaiah, Mishael, Malchijah, Hashum, Hashbadana, Zechariah, and Meshullam. And Ezra opened the book in the sight of all the people, for he was standing above all the people; and when he opened it, all the people stood up. And Ezra blessed the LORD, the great God.

Then all the people answered, "Amen, Amen!" while lifting up their hands. And they bowed their heads and worshiped the LORD with their faces to the ground.

Also Jeshua, Bani, Sherebiah, Jamin, Akkub, Shabbethai, Hodijah, Maaseiah, Kelita, Azariah, Jozabad, Hanan, Pelaiah, and the Levites, helped the people to understand the Law; and the people stood in their place. So they read distinctly from the book, in the Law of God; and they gave the sense, and helped them to understand the reading.

Ezra stood on that wooden pulpit and read the word of the Lord. When he got tired, another priest would take his place. And the people stood up all the time he was reading. This would take place from daylight until dark. We need to be thankful that the preachers of today give us a break from time to time.

Today we are all priests unto the Lord. 1 Peter 2:9 tells us,

But you are a chosen generation, a royal priesthood, a holy nation, His own special people, that you may proclaim the praises of Him who called you out of darkness into His marvelous light.

Here it is in The Amplified Bible: ***"But you are a chosen race, a royal priesthood, a dedicated nation, [God's] own purchased, special people, that you may set forth the wonderful deeds and display the virtues and perfection of Him Who called you out of darkness into His marvelous light."***

The Greek word for "peculiar" is represented best by a dot in a circle. That dot belongs to the circle. We are a people who belong to God. Our purpose is to proclaim abroad the message of life.

As priests, I believe we share the same role. We are to proclaim the word of God. All too often today, all we get are opinions. We listen to so many voices that we forget the power of His word. The church has lost its practice of teaching the Word of God.

I am so thankful for my Sunday School days. I learned not only the Bible stories, but also to love the scriptures. Today's church thrives on emotional roller coaster enthusiasm. There must be something exciting happening. We want to go where there are lights, sounds and action! If you announce you are having a Bible study, only a handful will respond. What a sad day for us. You mention the word doctrine and people's eyes glaze over. They don't want to study or hear the word taught line upon line.

Some of you have heard this funny story.

A young preacher appeared before the pulpit committee of a certain church. The chairman of the committee asked, "Young man, do you know your Bible?"

"Yes," the young man replied, "I know my Bible."

"What part do you know best?" the chairman asked.

The young preacher replied, "Well, I know it all good...the Old and New Testament."

The chairman said, "Well, why don't you tell us a story . . . how about the Good Samaritan?"

The young preacher replied that would be fine with him, so he began:

54

"There was a man of the Pharisees named Nicodemus who went down to Jericho by night and fell on stony ground, and the thorns choked him half to death. He said, 'What shall I do? I shall arise and go to my father's house.' And he arose and climbed into a sycamore tree."

"The next day, Solomon and his wife Gomorrah came by, and they carried him down to the ark for Moses to take care of. As he was going through the eastern gate of the ark, he caught his hair on a limb, and he hung there for 40 days and 40 nights. And afterwards he was hungry and the ravens came and fed him."

"The next day the three wise men came and carried him down to Ninevah, and when he got there, he found Delilah sitting on the wall, and he said, 'Chunk her down, boys,' and they said, 'How many times shall we chunk her down, 'til seven times?' And he said, 'Nay, but until 70 times 7.'

"So they chunked her down 490 times, and she burst asunder in their midst, and they picked up 12 baskets of the fragments that remained, and in the resurrection, whose wife will she be?"

After he had finished, the chairman of the committee turned to the other members and said, "I don't know about you, but I think we ought to call him. I know he is young, but he sure knows his Bible."

Now, while this has some humor in it, it also has a measure of truth about the church today. If a preacher preaches with gusto and says something loud enough and strong enough, some people will believe it. **We base our lives upon feelology and not theology.** People ask us today how we feel about something instead of what we believe about it.

It has become rare for doctrine to be the greatest importance in our churches. Experience cannot take the place of doctrine. The reason that salvation, healing, deliverance and the baptism in the Holy Spirit takes place in our lives does not come from our feelings, but the truth of the word of God.

Scripture tells us that the truth sets us free. We need the truth today. What we believe will change our lives and the lives of others. The purpose of doctrinal study is that it fills the need for an authoritative and systematic statement of truth.

The world says that it does not matter what a man believes so long as he does right. That is a lie. The Bible teaches us in Proverbs 14:12 that there is a way that seems right to a man, but the end is death. It is imperative that we know the truth.

- Doctrinal knowledge is essential to the full development of Christian behavior.
- It equips the believer to do good works (2 Timothy 3:16,17).
- It prepares the believer for effective warfare against satan (Matthew 4).
- It enables us to properly express love to the Lord and His people (1Timothy 1:5).
- It instructs us how to properly function in the House of the Lord (1 Timothy 3:14-15).

There is so much deception today. People are gullible and believe everything. We need consistent, sound teaching filled with the word of God to influence our lives.

We also proclaim the word with our lives. In 2 Corinthians Paul says,

"You are our epistle written in our hearts, known and read by all men." Part of our priesthood function is to proclaim the word of God with our lives. We are to be witnesses for Him in all that we do and say.

The church should be living out our message to the world. We must love the world and not condemn it. We must believe that God wants to bring reconciliation to people's lives. 1 Peter 2:9 says we have been "called out of darkness into His marvelous light." Thank God I have been called out of darkness. I know have a responsibility to share that message with anyone who will listen.

Evangelism is not *doing* as much as it is *being*. The scripture says in Acts 1:8 that we should *be* witnesses.

Many years ago I was traveling through a small rural city. There was a man standing in the city park with a sign strapped on him. He was a walking billboard. The front of the sign said, "**Repent or Perish**" and the back said, "**God Loves You**".

I was on my way to minister at a good church. I felt ashamed of this man who was unkempt and did not measure up to my standards. I spoke out my feelings to God. "I can't believe someone like him is representing your Kingdom." Immediately I felt God respond to me: "He is doing more for my Kingdom than you are."

I was devastated. I pulled to the side of the road and cried tears of repentance. The fact was while I was preaching to great churches; I had lost my desire to reach the lost wherever they were. I asked God to forgive me and open up doors to share His love with others. He has been faithful to do that.

This is a great time to share God's love. People are hungry for relationship. They are tired of religion. Let your light shine into the darkness of this world and believe Him for a harvest of souls. You need to believe that God put you where you are for His purposes. He believes in you and trusts you.

Don't let fear guide you, but have faith. I believe this is the greatest hour of the church. We will not lose this battle if we stay focused on our purpose. The driving force in our lives should be to proclaim to others that there is hope beyond where we are. Our message is not condemnation, but abundant life in Jesus Christ.

We are to offer sacrifices. Where there is a sanctuary, there must be a priesthood who offers sacrifices and oblations to God. These sacrifices are not the blood of bulls and goats, but of our lives. What are these sacrifices?

- **A sacrifice of Thanksgiving:** *Let them sacrifice the sacrifices of thanksgiving, And declare His works with rejoicing.* (Psalm 107:22)

- **A sacrifice of Joy:** *And now my head shall be lifted up above my enemies all around me. Therefore I will offer sacrifices of joy in His tabernacle. I will sing, yes, I will sing praises to the LORD* (Psalm 27:6)

- **A sacrifice of Praise:** *Therefore by Him let us continually offer the sacrifice of praise to God, that is, the fruit of our lips, giving thanks to His name.* (Hebrews 13:15)

- **A sacrifice of Obedience:** So Samuel said: *"Has the LORD as great delight in burnt offerings and sacrifices, As in obeying the voice of the LORD? Behold, to obey is better than sacrifice, and to heed than the fat of rams."* (1 Samuel 15:22)

- **A sacrifice of a broken spirit and righteousness:**
  For You do not desire sacrifice, or else I would give it;
  You do not delight in burnt offering.
  The sacrifices of God are a broken spirit,
  A broken and a contrite heart—
  These, O God, You will not despise.
  Do good in Your good pleasure to Zion;
  Build the walls of Jerusalem.
  Then You shall be pleased with the sacrifices of righteousness,
  With burnt offering and whole burnt offering;
  Then they shall offer bulls on Your altar.
  (Psalm 51:16-19)

- **A sacrifice of lifted hands:**
  LORD, I cry out to You;
  Make haste to me! Give ear to my voice
  when I cry out to You.
  Let my prayer be set before You be as
  incense,
  The lifting up of my hands as the evening
  sacrifice. (Psalm 141:1-2)
- **The sacrifice of our bodies and lives:**
  I beseech you therefore, brethren, by the
  mercies of God, that you present your bodies
  a living sacrifice, holy, acceptable to God,
  which is your reasonable service. And do
  not be conformed to this world, but be trans-
  formed by the renewing of your mind, that you
  may prove what is that good and acceptable
  and perfect will of God. (Romans 12:1-2)

Chapter 6:

The Porters

. . . and the porters   Nehemiah 10:39 KJV

In the middle of the priests and singers, the scripture mentions porters. Today we think of porters as those who help us carry luggage in airports. The word porter has two meanings in scripture. In Psalm 84:10 it is translated doorkeeper. That is a pretty simple task. Open and close doors all day as people enter and exit.

But it is also translated janitor. Those who keep things clean. Now isn't it amazing that the janitor would be in the middle of the priests and singers?

I believe the word carries the idea of servanthood. God wants us to know that it is a tremendous gift to be a servant. All places of ministry are not in the limelight. All places of ministry do not win the acclaim and the fame of men, nor get much applause. Some of the most needed ministry is not seen.

There were many feasts held in the Old Testament. These were special days when people came together and worshipped God. They read the scriptures. They sang songs of praise. They worshipped Him by offering sacrifices of bulls, goats, lambs and turtledoves.

Feasts were by divine decree of God. Animal sacrifices were a sign given to foretell the death of Jesus Christ. Even though we cannot fathom it today, they were a major part of life in the Old Testament. On feast days, the priests killed many animals. Not just one bull, but thousands of bulls, thousands of lambs and thousands of turtledoves. It was a very unpleasant sight.

I don't want to dwell here, but I do want you to get an idea of what happened. They slit the animals' throats, poured out their blood, put the carcasses on an altar of sacrifice and burned them. Not everything was consumed. The remains were placed in a pile. Multiply that by thousands of bulls, goats, lambs and turtledoves.

What a mess! Now the pictures we see portray these days without any mess. That is not the truth. After a day of sacrifice, everything was bloody and smelly. What did the priest do? He went to his tent to prepare for tomorrow's events.

Someone had to clean up the mess. Guess who got the job? The porter!

The priests went home. The people went to their tents. And the porters came out with the wheelbarrows. This was a dirty job. They dumped the animal remains in the wheelbarrows and took them outside the temple area. They went back in and wiped everything off. They left everything "spic and span" even though they did not have any of today's miracle cleaners. They used elbow grease. As they finished, daylight was approaching. The priests awakened, walked outside and shouted, "Bring on the bulls."

The priests did not have to clean up their mess. That was not their job. On certain days, they got really excited and dipped hyssop in the blood and sprinkled everything around with blood. They went back to their tents again and the porters came out to clean again.

I am sure that the porters may not have had many friends. Even if they cleaned up, everyone knew what they had been doing all night. They probably were not interested in having a meal. The good news is, the porters kept doing their job. If they quit, guess what would have happened? Conditions would have gone from bad to worse quickly. It would not have been pleasant. The porter did the work of the janitor. Ministry is not always being in the limelight.

We have to recognize that God has something for each of us to do. That is not easy for people to grasp today. We live in a star-minded society. We equate public speaking with ministry.

I attended a youth camp when I was a boy of 13 or 14, and God really stirred my soul. I was so inspired that when I went back to my home church, I said to the pastor, "I really want to do something for God." He never flinched. He said, "The storage room sure needs cleaning." I thought, "God, he didn't hear what I said. He must be confused."

Even though I was unsure of this plan, it did not matter. I was full of the Spirit. I went down to the storage room. It looked as though it had never been cleaned. It was thick with dirt and grime. I worked at it little by little and got it all squared away. I finally had it shining.

I went back to the pastor and said, "I got the storage room clean. I really want to do something for God. What can I do?" He said, "The basement sure could use painting." I could not believe this. I thought he would ask me to play the piano or sing a special in church as a reward for cleaning the storage room. Maybe give my testimony. But paint the basement? No!

But I did it. I cleaned everything up and painted it very nicely.

By this time, my spiritual fire had been quenched just a little. The next time I saw the pastor, I approached him in a different way. I still wanted to do something, but I wasn't sure he was getting the message. I just thought we were having a communication problem.

This time I said, "Pastor, there's nothing you want me to do, is there?" He said, "Yes there is. I really need the yard mowed." Now this was the last straw. I wanted to do something spiritual for the Kingdom and all he wanted me to do was clean the church.

While I was mowing, the Spirit spoke to me. He said, "If you do this for me, it is service to Me." I began to sing praises to the Lord. Thank you Jesus that I have legs to walk and arms to push. The more I praised Him, the more of His presence I felt.

The church today is desperate for people to help with the less glorious tasks. Most people are content to sit back Sunday after Sunday and desire blessings, but never want to be a blessing. People want to do things that are seen.

What a great gift it would be for people to start volunteering. It would almost be a miracle in some churches for people to be willing to serve in the obscure places. God keeps good records. He will honor those who do His will, regardless of the applause of men. We need all types of people to accomplish God's purpose. You may try to deny that you have talents and abilities God can use, but God knows every gift He has put in your life.

I realized when I was a pastor how many people it takes to make something happen. We must never take for granted those that serve in the nursery, the sound booth, setting up chairs, parking cars, etc. I have known people who were not known by others in the church. They were quiet and never bothered anyone. They were faithful to do God's will. I am glad that God keeps good records.

David said,

For a day in Your courts is better than a thousand (elsewhere).
I would rather be a doorkeeper in the house of my God
Than dwell in the tents of wickedness.
(Psalm 84:10)

What a great testimony. The word doorkeeper is the same word as porter. The passage could say that King David would rather be a janitor, clean up the mess of feast days, than dwell in the tents of the wicked. The tents of the wicked offered every conceivable pleasure of the day. David was saying he would rather take the lowest position in the Kingdom of God, than have the highest position in this world.

I would personally rather be in the lowest realm of things God offers than to have the greatest thing this world offers. I have had some pretty neat things happen to me through the years. I have had offers to do things that might bring the applause of men, but I have chosen to serve God with all my heart, soul, mind and strength.

I would rather have Jesus, His glory, His anointing and His purpose, simply to be what He wants me to be, than to have everything the world offers. An old song says, "To be like Jesus, to be like Jesus, All I ask, is to be like Him."

True success is serving. It has been said that the hardest position to fill in any orchestra is the second violin. But without it there is no harmony. Many today want positions that are seen of men, but God wants people who do His will and bring harmony to the church. Priests and singers are important in sharing the Kingdom of God, but I believe serving is the glue that holds everything together.

Some of you have been called as leadership gifts to the Body of Christ. You are an evangelist, pastor, apostle, prophet or teacher. Some of you are missionaries. God wants you to use your gift. You have held back for one reason or the other. God wants you to know that now is the time to put forth all your effort and to find your destiny.

Romans 12:1 says, present your bodies as living sacrifices. Whatever your gift is, use it for the glory of the Kingdom. **That brings me to something else we need to know**. Our service is not only to the house of God. Jesus left heaven to come to earth to serve those who had needs. He clearly states that His desire was not to be served, but to serve others. The church's mission to our planet is to serve those in need. It does not matter whether they are born again, go to church or even whether they are moral. Service reflects a genuine encounter with God. Pleasing God should be our highest priority. These scriptures tell us what God wants from us.

Isaiah 58:6-12

> 6 " *Is* this not the fast that I have chosen:
> To loose the bonds of wickedness,
> To undo the heavy burdens,
> To let the oppressed go free,
> And that you break every yoke?
> 7 *Is it* not to share your bread with the hungry,
> And that you bring to your house the poor who are cast out;
> When you see the naked, that you cover him,
> And not hide yourself from your own flesh?
> 8 Then your light shall break forth like the morning,

Your healing shall spring forth speedily,
And your righteousness shall go before you;
The glory of the LORD shall be your rear
guard.
9 Then you shall call, and the LORD will
answer;
You shall cry, and He will say, 'Here I *am*.'
" If you take away the yoke from your midst,
The pointing of the finger, and speaking
wickedness,
10 *If* you extend your soul to the hungry
And satisfy the afflicted soul,
Then your light shall dawn in the darkness,
And your darkness shall *be* as the noonday.
11 The LORD will guide you continually,
And satisfy your soul in drought,
And strengthen your bones;
You shall be like a watered garden,
And like a spring of water, whose waters do
not fail.
12 Those from among you
Shall build the old waste places;
You shall raise up the foundations of many
generations;
And you shall be called the Repairer of the
Breach,
The Restorer of Streets to Dwell In.

How often do we help people in our neighbor-
hood? Do we take time to just surprise people with
the love of God. I remember one lesson from a friend
who would just periodically buy someone lunch

anonymously. I know these acts of kindness touch people's lives and softens their hearts. I urge you to look for ways to reach out and be a blessing. The Kingdom of God encompasses more than our local church, our friends, our relationships. It involves people from every walk of life. Some of them are closer to the Kingdom than we know. A simple act of kindness can be the catalyst to move a little closer to the presence of the Lord. Jesus said this in the New Testament.

Matthew 25:34-46

34 Then the King will say to those on His right hand, 'Come, you blessed of My Father, inherit the kingdom prepared for you from the foundation of the world: 35 for I was hungry and you gave Me food; I was thirsty and you gave Me drink; I was a stranger and you took Me in; 36 I *was* naked and you clothed Me; I was sick and you visited Me; I was in prison and you came to Me.'

37 "Then the righteous will answer Him, saying, 'Lord, when did we see You hungry and feed *You,* or thirsty and give *You* drink? 38 When did we see You a stranger and take *You* in, or naked and clothe *You?* 39 Or when did we see You sick, or in prison, and come to You?' 40 And the King will answer and say to them, 'Assuredly, I say to you, inasmuch as you did *it* to one of the least of these My brethren, you did *it* to Me.'

41 "Then He will also say to those on the left hand, 'Depart from Me, you cursed, into the everlasting fire prepared for the devil and his angels: 42 for I was

hungry and you gave Me no food; I was thirsty and you gave Me no drink; 43 I was a stranger and you did not take Me in, naked and you did not clothe Me, sick and in prison and you did not visit Me.'

44 "Then they also will answer Him,[a] saying, 'Lord, when did we see You hungry or thirsty or a stranger or naked or sick or in prison, and did not minister to You?' 45 Then He will answer them, saying, 'Assuredly, I say to you, inasmuch as you did not do *it* to one of the least of these, you did not do *it* to Me.' 46 And these will go away into everlasting punishment, but the righteous into eternal life."

The main idea here is that we can not overlook touching those in need. We stand in a place of caring and able to show the love of God in meaningful ways. I urge you to find a place of service. Prisons, nursing homes, and orphanages are all in need of practical service from the people of God. Be a porter and use your gifts with a heart of gratitude to those who are in need.

Chapter 7:

The Singers

. . . and the singers   Nehemiah 10:39 KJV

Thank God for the singers. Thank God for those who have a song in their heart. Thank God for those who are not there because of habit, not there to go through the motions, not there to have their programs, but are there to sing a song unto the Lord. Why? Because He is Worthy! God desires our praises. He wants our love.

It amazes me how some people can go out of the church where the Glory of God has moved in a powerful way and all they can do is say, "Woe is me." I wonder if they were in the same meeting I had just been in. We had just come from a place of power. We had touched the Lord, but more important, He had touched us. We should exit with a note of victory. We have been given a new song that flows from the river inside us.

I cannot keep from praising the Lord. I must praise Him. I am thankful for all the songs that have ever been written, but sometimes I must sing a new song to Him that shares my heart.

Why do we praise the Lord? 1 Peter 2:9 says, *"But you are a chosen race, a royal priesthood, a dedicated nation, (God's) own purchased, special people, that you may set forth the wonderful deeds and display the virtues and perfections of Him Who called you out of darkness into His marvelous light."* The Amplified Bible

We praise Him because of who we are. We are a holy race. The royal blood of Jesus runs through my veins. I am now a partaker of all the riches and glories of God. I am a child of the living God. I've been bought with the blood of Jesus Christ. I have been set apart. I am abiding in the Vine. I am an heir of the Father and a joint heir with Jesus Christ. The seed of Abraham has been placed within my life. I am a new creation!!

So many people act as though their relationship with Christ is something they don't want anyone to know about. They consider it to be a second rate citizenship. They walk with their heads bowed and cross to the other side of the road when they see someone coming. They seem to feel inferior.

We should let the world know, *"I am a Christian, I follow Jesus Christ! He is the Lord and Savior of my life."* He has called us with a Holy calling. Jesus loved Ronald Gray enough that to look out through the eternal ages, see me, and choose to die for me so that I can have everlasting, abundant life. He did the same for you and everyone on this planet.

We also worship God because of *what* we are. We are King-Priests. We are priests unto God. He called each and every one of us to the priesthood. We all have the ability to sacrifice. We all can go into the Holy of Holies because the veil has been torn in two. We all can offer sacrifices of praise and worship to God because of the One who died for us on the cross of Calvary.

We also praise Him because of *where* we are. We are a Holy nation. The definition of nation is, "A group of people that come under one government; a group of people set apart by boundaries." We come under the rule and reign (the government) of Jesus Christ. He is our Controller. He is our Master. He is Wonderful, the Mighty God, the Prince of Peace and the Everlasting Father.

We have only one God. We follow Him with all diligence. We believe that He is represented through the Father, Son and Holy Spirit, but we believe He is one God. We are not interested in man's opinion. We are not here to listen to the world's opinions. We want to follow the leadership of the Holy Spirit.

We have boundaries. While we walk in liberty, we are still people who are in this world, but not of it. Holiness is still God's plan. We need to study that word. The Bible tells us we will not see God without being holy. Holiness is not religious attitudes contrived by people, but a position that God wants us to hold by faith.

I grew up under some pretty strict guidelines. My salvation was defined by what I did not do, where I did not go and how I did not dress. Thank God for liberty, but liberty is not a license to sin.

We are not here to please self. There is a cult of self that has invaded many of our churches. We seek to please ourselves rather than God. There are still commandments and direction for our lives. Our desire should be to live at the center of His will. We want to honor the Lord with our living.

We praise Him because of how we came to be. The scripture says we are a people formed for God's own possession, to tell of the One who called us out of darkness into everlasting light.

It is still wonderful to sing, "Amazing grace, how sweet the sound, that saved a wretch like me." I was not worthy to be saved. I had nothing to contribute to the Kingdom of God, but He loved me anyway. He gave His life for me on the cross of Calvary. That is the reason we praise Him. He did not have to do it. He did it out of love.

Other religions hope to gain entrance to heaven and riches and glory on earth by doing good works, by going to the right places, by saying the right things and by doing what they think is right. We cannot boast in our own efforts. It is "Not by works, lest any man should boast." Thank God that He is merciful to us in our ignorance. It is never through anything I can do or give. It is all by Him, of Him, through Him and because of Him that I have life eternal.

I believe that Jesus saw me through the ages as He hung on the cross and said, "I am dying for you so that you can have everlasting life."

When we exit the house of God, we should be singing the songs of Zion. We should sing the song that angels cannot sing. The song of the redeemed. The scriptures declare that we should sing a new song. We need a melody in our hearts.

Psalm 96:1-13 (King James Version):
Oh, sing to the LORD a new song!
Sing to the LORD, all the earth.
Sing to the LORD, bless His name;
Proclaim the good news of His salvation from day to day.
Declare His glory among the nations,
His wonders among all peoples.

For the LORD is great and greatly to be praised;
He is to be feared above all gods.
For all the gods of the peoples are idols,
But the LORD made the heavens.
Honor and majesty are before Him;
Strength and beauty are in His sanctuary.

Give to the LORD, O families of the peoples,
Give to the LORD glory and strength.
Give to the LORD the glory due His name;
Bring an offering, and come into His courts.

*Oh, worship the LORD in the beauty of
holiness!
Tremble before Him, all the earth.*

*Say among the nations, "The LORD reigns;
The world also is firmly established,
It shall not be moved;
He shall judge the peoples righteously."*

*Let the heavens rejoice, and let the earth be glad;
Let the sea roar, and all its fullness;
Let the field be joyful, and all that is in it.
Then all the trees of the woods will rejoice
before the LORD.
For He is coming, for He is coming to judge the
earth.
He shall judge the world with righteousness,
And the peoples with His truth.*

Psalm 103:1-5(King James Version):

*Bless the LORD, O my soul;
and all that is within me, bless his holy name.
Bless the LORD, O my soul,
and forget not all his benefits:
Who forgiveth all thine iniquities;
who healeth all thy diseases;
Who redeemeth thy life from destruction;
who crowneth thee with lovingkindness and
tender mercies;
Who satisfieth thy mouth with good things;
so that thy youth is renewed like the eagle's.*

Psalm 104:1-3 (King James Version):

Bless the LORD, O my soul. O LORD my God, thou art very great; thou art clothed with honour and majesty.
Who coverest thyself with light as with a garment: who stretchest out the heavens like a curtain:
Who layeth the beams of his chambers in the waters: who maketh the clouds his chariot: who walketh upon the wings of the wind.

This is what the Lord desires from us. We have a song. We all are appointed singers unto God. Let the Glory of the Lord fill us and consume us. Let us not leave His house with a song of the blues, or a song of defeat. We should go forth with the praises of God on our lips. Don't allow the enemy to rob you of your song. There is a river of life in you. Let it flow. When you do this, you will find a strength that you never imagined.

Some are afraid to sing a new song unto the Lord, either in English or in the Spirit. That fear is not from God. Paul says, *"For God has not given us a spirit of fear, but of power and of love and of a sound mind."* (2 Timothy 1:7)

When you sing a new song, it will be as the sound of many waters. That is the voice of God. People will ask where the sound comes from. The many waters produce the voice of God in our midst. God wants to reveal Himself to us more than we can imagine. I love this scripture in 2 Chronicles 5:11-14:

And it came to pass when the priests came out of the Most Holy Place (for all the priests who were present had sanctified themselves, without keeping to their divisions), and the Levites who were the singers, all those of Asaph and Heman and Jeduthun, with their sons and their brethren, stood at the east end of the altar, clothed in white linen, having cymbals, stringed instruments and harps, and with them one hundred and twenty priests sounding with trumpets— indeed it came to pass, when the trumpeters and singers were as one, to make one sound to be heard in praising and thanking the LORD, and when they lifted up their voice with the trumpets and cymbals and instruments of music, and praised the LORD, saying:

"For He is good,

For His mercy endures forever,"

that the house, the house of the LORD, was filled with a cloud, so that the priests could not continue ministering because of the cloud; for the glory of the LORD filled the house of God.

God wants to fill His house with Glory. He wants to use us in ways we have never dreamed.

Another powerful scripture of singing is 2 Chronicles 20:17-22:

"'You will not need to fight in this battle. Position yourselves, stand still and see the salvation of the LORD, who is with you, O Judah and Jerusalem!'

Do not fear or be dismayed; tomorrow go out against them, for the LORD is with you."

And Jehoshaphat bowed his head with his face to the ground, and all Judah and the inhabitants of Jerusalem bowed before the LORD, worshiping the LORD. Then the Levites of the children of the Kohathites and of the children of the Korahites stood up to praise the LORD God of Israel with voices loud and high.

So they rose early in the morning and went out into the Wilderness of Tekoa; and as they went out, Jehoshaphat stood and said, "Hear me, O Judah and you inhabitants of Jerusalem: Believe in the LORD your God, and you shall be established; believe His prophets, and you shall prosper." And when he had consulted with the people, he appointed those who should sing to the LORD, and who should praise the beauty of holiness, as they went out before the army and were saying:

"Praise the LORD,

For His mercy endures forever."

Now when they began to sing and to praise, the LORD set ambushes against the people of Ammon, Moab, and Mount Seir, who had come against Judah; and they were defeated."

We see a picture that, after the Glory of the Lord had filled the temple, the men of Judah realized a few chapters later that they were still in a war. They appointed the singers to go before the army. No spears, no swords, just singers. When they went forward,

God took over and gave them the victory. There is a tendency to wait till we have all the answers to praise the Lord. God desires our praise to lead the way.

We must trust in the Lord. We are here to take the land God has deeded to us by inheritance. We are not to do this in our own strength. We are not here to fight in the power of our flesh. We declare to the world that our trust is in the God who is Alpha and Omega. Start singing the song of the Lord. Sing out of your heart. Sing to the world that God is still God.

Worship is not just for the choir and musicians. Some people have the attitude that singers are frail and uptight. God said He wanted people of praise at the front of the army. The truth is that when we obey God, He fights our battles for us. People ask what we did. We tell them we sang and gave praise to God. We realize that it is all Him.

As the Lord told Zechariah,
So he answered and said to me:
"This is the word of the LORD to Zerubbabel:
'Not by might nor by power, but by My Spirit,'
Says the LORD of hosts. (Zechariah 4:6)

Is it our place to take on the world in debates? Are we going to condemn all those who don't agree with us? No! We will just keep singing our song. The song of the redeemed. God will conquer every enemy, shake every prison door and give us victory in our lives. It is time for God's Spirit to fill His house and let the world know once again that He is God Almighty!

So, by sacrifice and obedience and by praise we will EXIT TO SERVE!

Conclusion

There is within every one of us a self-centered attitude that keeps us from fulfilling our potential in Christ. We can overcome that self-centeredness by focusing our lives on what is productive living in the Kingdom of God. The Church was designed by our Father to be effective. We are here to make a difference in society and family. I urge you to find ways to worship God, be filled with His presence and then serve Him in your daily lives. We can accomplish the mission that God has given us if we follow His plan. May God help us in our endeavors!

I pray this book helps you to do some things different in your life. The easiest thing for all of us to do is just continue the way we are. We don't want to make the effort to discipline ourselves in the ways of God. I urge you to take some of these principles today and begin to work them out in your life. Take the opportunity to trust God in these areas. I believe it will be life changing.

If you need prayer or just want to share a testimony, please contact us at:

Ronald Gray Ministries
P.O. Box 1873
Daphne, AL 36526

251-621-0983
RonaldKGray@aol.com
RonaldGrayMinistries.org

If you would like to order more books, please contact our office.